PRINCEWILL LAGANG

The Gig Economy Entrepreneur:
Thriving as a Freelancer

First published by PRINCEWILL LAGANG 2023

Copyright © 2023 by Princewill Lagang

All rights reserved. No part of this publication may be reproduced, stored or transmitted in any form or by any means, electronic, mechanical, photocopying, recording, scanning, or otherwise without written permission from the publisher. It is illegal to copy this book, post it to a website, or distribute it by any other means without permission.

Princewill Lagang asserts the moral right to be identified as the author of this work.

First edition

This book was professionally typeset on Reedsy.
Find out more at reedsy.com

Contents

1. The Gig Economy Entrepreneur: Thriving as a Freelancer — 1
2. Building Your Brand: Crafting an Irresistible Freelance... — 4
3. The Art of Freelance Pricing: Maximizing Earnings and Value — 7
4. Securing and Managing Clients: The Key to Sustainable... — 10
5. Mastering Your Craft: Continuous Learning and Professional... — 13
6. Financial Mastery: Managing Your Freelance Finances Like a... — 16
7. Work-Life Balance and Self-Care: Nurturing Your Well-Being — 19
8. Scaling Your Freelance Business: Growing Beyond the Solo Act — 22
9. Navigating Challenges and Overcoming Setbacks — 25
10. Leaving a Legacy and Giving Back — 28
11. Embracing Change and Adaptation in the Gig Economy — 31
12. Reflection and Future Horizons — 34

1

The Gig Economy Entrepreneur: Thriving as a Freelancer

The morning sun cast a warm glow across the city as Sarah's alarm jolted her awake. She reached for her phone, swiping off the ringing sound and squinting at the time. 6:30 AM. Another day had begun, and Sarah was about to embark on her journey as a gig economy entrepreneur, a path she had chosen with enthusiasm and a hint of trepidation.

For Sarah, and for countless others around the world, the gig economy represented a new way of working, one defined by independence, flexibility, and the promise of economic prosperity. But in the rapidly changing landscape of the 21st century, it also posed challenges and uncertainties. Chapter 1 of "The Gig Economy Entrepreneur: Thriving as a Freelancer" delves into the heart of this evolving landscape, exploring the opportunities, pitfalls, and strategies that freelancers and independent workers need to navigate to succeed.

The Rise of the Gig Economy

THE GIG ECONOMY ENTREPRENEUR: THRIVING AS A FREELANCER

The gig economy, also known as the freelance or on-demand economy, had undergone an unprecedented explosion over the past two decades. It transformed the traditional notion of a stable, 9-to-5 job into a diverse spectrum of work arrangements. From software developers and graphic designers to drivers and delivery couriers, millions of individuals now earned their livelihoods through short-term contracts, projects, or part-time jobs.

This seismic shift was driven by a convergence of factors. Advances in technology, particularly the proliferation of internet connectivity and the rise of digital platforms, had made it easier than ever to match freelancers with clients. People were increasingly seeking flexibility and autonomy in their work, and businesses were eager to tap into specialized skills without the burden of long-term employment commitments. The gig economy provided the perfect solution for both parties.

The Promise and Peril

As Sarah stared at her reflection in the bathroom mirror, she contemplated the dual nature of the gig economy. On one hand, it offered the promise of freedom, allowing individuals to set their own schedules, choose their clients, and work from anywhere in the world. Sarah was no longer confined to a cubicle, and she relished the thought of spending more time with her family while pursuing her passion for graphic design.

However, the gig economy also brought with it a host of challenges. The absence of traditional employment benefits such as health insurance and retirement plans meant freelancers had to manage their own finances and wellbeing. Competition was fierce, and the constant need to market oneself and secure new projects could be exhausting. The feast-or-famine nature of freelancing meant that, while some months might be lucrative, others could be lean.

In "The Gig Economy Entrepreneur," we explore the strategies and tools that individuals like Sarah can use to navigate these challenges and maximize the opportunities the gig economy provides.

The Gig Economy Mindset

Sarah finished getting ready and headed to her home office, a corner of her living room furnished with a desk, a comfortable chair, and an array of computer screens. She had been living the gig economy life for a while now and had learned that success in this world required more than just a specific skill set. It required a mindset, a way of thinking that embraced change and embraced risk.

Chapter 1 explores the essential qualities of a gig economy entrepreneur, including adaptability, resilience, and a growth mindset. It delves into the art of self-discipline, setting goals, and managing time effectively. Sarah's journey would become a case study in how to thrive in this rapidly evolving world.

As "The Gig Economy Entrepreneur" unfolds, we will accompany Sarah on her quest for success, and together, we will discover the wisdom, strategies, and insights that can help freelancers not only survive but truly thrive in the gig economy. The journey begins with this chapter, as we lay the foundation for a fulfilling and prosperous life as a freelancer.

2

Building Your Brand: Crafting an Irresistible Freelance Profile

As the sun streamed through her window, Sarah found herself sitting in front of her computer, coffee in hand, ready to embark on the next step of her gig economy journey. Chapter 2 of "The Gig Economy Entrepreneur: Thriving as a Freelancer" would be all about building her brand, crafting a freelance profile that would attract clients like bees to honey.

The Power of Your Brand

Sarah had a distinct style and a unique approach to graphic design, but she realized that her talents alone were not enough. In the gig economy, success hinged on her ability to stand out in a crowded marketplace. As she sipped her coffee, she contemplated the power of her brand, and the profound impact it would have on her freelancing career.

A brand wasn't just a logo or a catchy slogan; it was the essence of who she was as a freelancer. It conveyed her values, her expertise, and the promises she made to her clients. A strong brand, she understood, was a magnet for clients who resonated with her vision and her work.

Defining Your Unique Selling Proposition

To build a compelling brand, Sarah needed to define her Unique Selling Proposition (USP). What made her different from the myriad other graphic designers in the gig economy? She delved into a process of self-reflection, identifying her strengths, passions, and the particular niche within graphic design that set her apart.

Chapter 2 would guide Sarah through this introspective journey, helping her distill her USP into a clear, concise message that would serve as the foundation of her freelance brand. She learned that being specific and authentic was key to attracting the right clients who would value her unique skills and perspective.

The Freelance Profile

One of the first and most crucial steps in building a brand as a gig economy entrepreneur was creating a standout profile on the platforms and websites where she would find clients. Sarah logged into her freelance marketplace accounts and examined her existing profiles.

Chapter 2 provided Sarah with detailed insights into optimizing her profile. It covered everything from selecting the right profile picture and crafting a compelling bio to showcasing her portfolio and earning client reviews. Sarah realized that her profile was not just an online resume; it was a dynamic representation of her brand. It had to tell her story and demonstrate her capabilities in a way that resonated with potential clients.

Portfolio Development

Sarah's portfolio was her showcase to the world. It was where she could display her skills, creativity, and the quality of her work. In this chapter, Sarah explored the art of portfolio development. She discovered how to curate and present her best work, highlighting projects that exemplified her USP and appealed to her target audience.

Through the book's guidance, Sarah would learn the importance of consistency in her portfolio, how to explain her creative process, and why storytelling played a crucial role in connecting with potential clients. She realized that a well-crafted portfolio would not only attract clients but also communicate her professional credibility and reliability.

As she continued to refine her brand and freelance profile, Sarah understood that this was a transformative journey. Chapter 2 was just the beginning, setting the stage for her success as a gig economy entrepreneur. Building her brand and crafting an irresistible freelance profile were essential steps on the path to thriving in the ever-evolving world of freelancing.

3

The Art of Freelance Pricing: Maximizing Earnings and Value

Sarah had invested considerable time and effort into building her freelance brand and crafting a compelling profile. With each passing day, she was more confident in her ability to attract clients. However, as she sat down to delve into Chapter 3 of "The Gig Economy Entrepreneur: Thriving as a Freelancer," she knew that success was not solely about securing projects; it was also about pricing those projects in a way that was fair to both her and her clients.

Pricing Psychology

Pricing was more than just numbers on a page; it was a psychological game. Sarah learned that her pricing strategy could influence a client's perception of her value and professionalism. In this chapter, she would uncover the subtle nuances of pricing psychology and how to use them to her advantage.

She delved into the concepts of anchoring, framing, and tiered pricing. She learned how to present her rates in a way that made clients feel they were getting a good deal while also allowing her to maximize her earnings. Sarah knew that setting the right price was an art, and Chapter 3 would be her canvas.

Cost Analysis

Before setting her prices, Sarah realized she needed to have a solid understanding of her own costs. She couldn't simply pick a number out of thin air. Her pricing needed to cover her expenses, provide her with a reasonable income, and still remain competitive in the market.

In this chapter, Sarah examined her costs methodically. She considered her living expenses, business overhead, taxes, and savings goals. She also took into account the competitive landscape, researching what other freelancers with similar skill sets and experience were charging. Armed with this information, she would be ready to set her prices with confidence.

Value-Based Pricing

Sarah believed that her work was not just about delivering a service; it was about delivering value. In the gig economy, clients often valued results over the hours worked. Chapter 3 introduced Sarah to the concept of value-based pricing, where she would align her prices with the outcomes her clients expected to achieve.

She learned that value-based pricing allowed her to focus on the unique benefits she provided to each client. It allowed her to have a conversation with clients about the return on investment they could expect from her services. By understanding her clients' pain points and business goals, Sarah could charge a premium for her expertise and the results she would deliver.

Pricing Models

Sarah was also introduced to different pricing models. Whether it was hourly rates, project-based pricing, or retainer contracts, she needed to choose the model that best suited her and her clients. Each model had its pros and cons, and Chapter 3 provided a comprehensive guide to help her make an informed decision.

She discovered that some projects were best suited for fixed pricing, while others required hourly rates. The flexibility of retainer contracts allowed her to build long-term relationships with clients. By the end of the chapter, Sarah would have a clear understanding of when to use each pricing model to her advantage.

As Sarah delved into Chapter 3, she was excited to transform her understanding of pricing. She knew that mastering the art of freelance pricing was not only about maximizing her earnings but also about delivering the best value to her clients. This chapter would set her on the path to becoming a financially savvy and successful gig economy entrepreneur.

4

Securing and Managing Clients: The Key to Sustainable Freelance Success

The hustle and bustle of Sarah's freelance life had intensified as she put into practice the valuable lessons from the previous chapters. With her brand established and pricing strategy refined, she knew that the next step in her journey, as detailed in Chapter 4 of "The Gig Economy Entrepreneur: Thriving as a Freelancer," was to secure and manage clients effectively, the lifeblood of her freelance career.

Finding Your Ideal Clients

For Sarah, it was not just about attracting any client; it was about attracting the right clients. She understood that successful freelancers built their reputations and networks by working with clients who valued their expertise. Chapter 4 began with a deep dive into finding and identifying her ideal clients.

She learned how to create detailed client personas and understand their pain points, needs, and motivations. By honing in on the clients she wanted to work with, Sarah would be able to tailor her marketing efforts and approach to attract those who resonated with her unique offering.

Marketing and Outreach

Sarah's freelancing journey was about more than just creating a profile and waiting for clients to find her. She needed to be proactive in marketing her services. This chapter introduced her to a range of marketing strategies, from social media and content marketing to networking and referrals.

Sarah embraced the art of storytelling in her marketing efforts, using her brand narrative to connect with potential clients on a personal level. The chapter also offered insights into building a compelling portfolio website, crafting effective pitches, and using digital platforms to her advantage. By the end, she would have a comprehensive toolkit for attracting clients in the gig economy.

Client Relationships

Securing a client was just the beginning. Managing and nurturing client relationships were equally important to ensure repeat business and referrals. Sarah delved into the intricacies of building strong client relationships in Chapter 4. She learned about the importance of communication, setting clear expectations, and delivering value consistently.

The chapter also explored the art of effective client onboarding, creating service agreements, and handling difficult clients or challenging situations. Sarah was determined to turn her clients into long-term partners who not only appreciated her work but also trusted her as a reliable and professional freelancer.

Time Management and Scaling

As Sarah's client base grew, she realized the need for efficient time management and scaling her freelance business. Chapter 4 provided valuable insights into time management techniques, such as the Pomodoro technique, time blocking, and task prioritization. These strategies would help her balance her work and personal life while maintaining a high level of productivity.

She also learned about the art of scaling her freelance business by outsourcing tasks or expanding her services. The chapter touched on hiring virtual assistants, subcontracting, or partnering with other freelancers to take on larger projects. Sarah understood that scaling required careful planning and a strong foundation.

By the end of Chapter 4, Sarah felt more equipped than ever to secure, manage, and nurture her client relationships effectively. She knew that clients were not just projects but partners in her journey to thrive in the gig economy. As her confidence grew, so did her potential for long-term success as a freelance entrepreneur.

5

Mastering Your Craft: Continuous Learning and Professional Growth

Sarah's journey in the gig economy was nothing short of a transformation. With her brand established, a well-defined pricing strategy, and a growing list of satisfied clients, she had come a long way. As she delved into Chapter 5 of "The Gig Economy Entrepreneur: Thriving as a Freelancer," she was eager to explore the importance of continuous learning and professional growth in her evolving career.

Embracing Lifelong Learning

One thing Sarah had quickly realized about freelancing was that it demanded adaptability. The gig economy was ever-evolving, with new technologies and trends emerging at a rapid pace. Chapter 5 began with a deep dive into the concept of lifelong learning.

Sarah learned that to thrive as a freelancer, she needed to continuously update her skills and knowledge. The chapter introduced her to a range of learning opportunities, from online courses and workshops to webinars and industry conferences. She understood that investing in her education was an investment in her future.

Networking and Mentorship

In the gig economy, relationships were just as important as skills. Sarah discovered the power of networking and mentorship as she explored Chapter 5. She learned that networking wasn't just about collecting business cards; it was about building meaningful connections with fellow freelancers, industry professionals, and potential clients.

Mentorship was another valuable resource for her growth. Sarah realized that having a mentor could provide her with guidance, insights, and a fresh perspective on her career. The chapter offered tips on finding and building relationships with mentors who could help her navigate the freelancing landscape.

Building a Personal Brand

Sarah's personal brand was not a static entity; it was something that evolved along with her skills and experiences. In this chapter, she uncovered the importance of updating her personal brand to reflect her professional growth. She learned about reevaluating her Unique Selling Proposition (USP), refreshing her portfolio, and showcasing her ongoing learning experiences.

The chapter also emphasized the value of sharing her knowledge with her audience. Blogging, speaking engagements, or creating educational content were all ways for her to position herself as an expert in her field. By demonstrating her expertise, she would be more likely to attract high-value clients and exciting projects.

Setting Goals and Tracking Progress

As Sarah's career progressed, setting and tracking her goals became crucial.

Chapter 5 introduced her to the art of SMART goals (Specific, Measurable, Achievable, Relevant, and Time-bound) and how to use them to guide her professional development. She understood that by setting clear objectives, she could measure her progress and stay motivated.

Sarah also learned about the importance of self-assessment and performance reviews. Periodically evaluating her work, client feedback, and personal achievements helped her identify areas for improvement and further growth. It also allowed her to recognize her successes and celebrate her milestones.

As she absorbed the wisdom of Chapter 5, Sarah knew that the journey of professional growth in the gig economy was a continuous one. She was excited to embrace lifelong learning, build valuable relationships, and elevate her personal brand as she moved forward. With each step, she was one step closer to becoming a true gig economy entrepreneur, thriving in a dynamic and ever-evolving world.

6

Financial Mastery: Managing Your Freelance Finances Like a Pro

As Sarah's freelance career continued to flourish, she recognized the importance of not only earning money but also managing it wisely. In Chapter 6 of "The Gig Economy Entrepreneur: Thriving as a Freelancer," Sarah delved into the world of financial mastery to ensure that her finances were secure, organized, and optimized for long-term success.

Financial Planning and Budgeting

Sarah knew that as a freelancer, her income could be variable. In this chapter, she learned the art of financial planning and budgeting. She started by defining her financial goals, whether they were short-term, like paying off debt, or long-term, like saving for retirement. Once she had a clear vision, she could create a budget that would help her achieve those goals.

The chapter introduced her to budgeting tools and strategies, emphasizing the importance of tracking expenses and setting aside a portion of her income for taxes and savings. She understood that financial planning was the foundation of her financial security.

Taxes and Deductions

As a gig economy entrepreneur, Sarah was responsible for managing her taxes, which could be complex due to self-employment income. Chapter 6 covered the essentials of tax planning and compliance. Sarah learned how to keep detailed records, understand tax deductions, and estimate her quarterly tax payments.

The chapter also explained the value of working with an accountant or tax professional, who could help her navigate the intricacies of the tax code and ensure she was maximizing her deductions while staying in compliance with tax laws.

Retirement and Investments

Sarah realized that, unlike traditional employees, she didn't have access to an employer-sponsored retirement plan. In this chapter, she explored various retirement savings options available to freelancers, such as individual retirement accounts (IRAs) and simplified employee pension (SEP) plans.

She also delved into the world of investing. Sarah discovered how to grow her wealth by diversifying her investments, understanding risk tolerance, and building a balanced portfolio. By the end of the chapter, she had a clear roadmap for securing her financial future.

Emergency Fund and Insurance

The chapter emphasized the importance of building an emergency fund. Sarah learned how to set aside a portion of her income in a high-yield savings account to cover unexpected expenses or periods of low income. Having an emergency fund provided her with financial security and peace of mind.

Additionally, the chapter discussed the value of insurance, including health, disability, and liability insurance. Sarah understood that insurance was a vital component of her financial plan, protecting her from unexpected health costs or legal issues that could arise in her freelance work.

As Sarah absorbed the insights of Chapter 6, she knew that mastering her freelance finances was not just about making money but also about managing it wisely. Financial security and independence were within her reach, and she was determined to achieve them, armed with the knowledge and strategies to navigate the financial complexities of the gig economy.

7

Work-Life Balance and Self-Care: Nurturing Your Well-Being

Sarah had come a long way in her journey as a gig economy entrepreneur. She had built her brand, mastered pricing, secured clients, continued her professional growth, and managed her finances like a pro. In Chapter 7 of "The Gig Economy Entrepreneur: Thriving as a Freelancer," she delved into an equally crucial aspect of her career—nurturing her well-being and maintaining a healthy work-life balance.

The Importance of Work-Life Balance

Sarah had experienced the thrill of freelancing but had also encountered its challenges, including the tendency to overwork and burnout. Chapter 7 began by emphasizing the importance of work-life balance. She learned that balancing work and personal life was not just a luxury but a necessity for her long-term success and well-being.

The chapter introduced her to the potential consequences of a poor work-life balance, such as decreased productivity, increased stress, and strained personal relationships. Sarah was determined to avoid these pitfalls and achieve equilibrium in her life.

Setting Boundaries

As a freelancer, it was easy to be always "on." In this chapter, Sarah explored the art of setting boundaries. She learned to define her working hours and personal time, communicating these boundaries to her clients and herself.

The chapter provided practical strategies for establishing boundaries, such as turning off work notifications after hours, designating a dedicated workspace, and scheduling regular breaks. Sarah realized that setting boundaries was an essential step in protecting her well-being and maintaining a healthy work-life balance.

Self-Care

Self-care was a recurring theme in Chapter 7. Sarah discovered the value of taking care of her physical, mental, and emotional health. The chapter emphasized the importance of regular exercise, a balanced diet, and sufficient sleep.

Sarah also learned to recognize and manage stress. She explored relaxation techniques, mindfulness practices, and ways to unplug and recharge. The chapter underscored the significance of self-care as a foundation for her overall well-being.

Time Management for Balance

Balancing work and personal life required effective time management. The chapter introduced Sarah to time management techniques that would help her achieve her goals while also making time for her personal life.

She learned about the Pomodoro Technique, time blocking, and prioritization. These strategies allowed her to work more efficiently, freeing up time for activities that brought her joy and relaxation. Sarah realized that time management was the key to maintaining her desired balance.

Evaluating Progress

Chapter 7 closed with a discussion on evaluating progress. Sarah learned to assess her work-life balance periodically, making necessary adjustments when needed. She realized that work-life balance was an ongoing process, and her needs and priorities might evolve over time.

Sarah was determined to make her well-being a priority and to create a sustainable freelance career that allowed her to thrive both professionally and personally. With the insights and strategies from Chapter 7, she felt better equipped to achieve a harmonious work-life balance and take care of herself in the demanding world of the gig economy.

8

Scaling Your Freelance Business: Growing Beyond the Solo Act

Sarah's journey in the gig economy had been filled with challenges, triumphs, and continuous learning. As she opened Chapter 8 of "The Gig Economy Entrepreneur: Thriving as a Freelancer," she was excited to explore the possibilities of scaling her freelance business, taking it to the next level, and potentially expanding beyond the solo act.

The Desire for Growth

Sarah had come a long way from her early days as a solo freelancer. She had honed her skills, built a strong brand, and secured a loyal client base. In this chapter, she contemplated the desire for growth and the potential for expanding her freelance business.

The chapter began by helping Sarah assess her readiness for growth, both professionally and personally. She learned to recognize the signs that indicated it might be time to scale her business. Sarah was ready to explore the possibilities of expansion.

Building a Team

To scale her freelance business, Sarah knew that she might need help. In Chapter 8, she delved into the world of building a team, whether through hiring employees, collaborating with other freelancers, or outsourcing specific tasks.

The chapter provided Sarah with valuable insights into the hiring process, including defining job roles, conducting interviews, and onboarding team members. She also learned about the benefits and challenges of working with other freelancers or subcontractors. Sarah understood that building a capable team was a critical step in achieving growth.

Managing Finances and Operations

Scaling a freelance business came with financial and operational challenges. Sarah explored strategies for managing the financial aspects of growth, including setting up business structures, creating budgets, and securing additional financing if necessary.

She also learned about operational considerations, such as workflow optimization, project management, and client relationship management as her business expanded. The chapter emphasized the importance of efficient systems and processes to support growth.

Marketing and Sales

Scaling a freelance business required effective marketing and sales strategies. Sarah delved into the art of marketing her expanded services and products to a broader audience. She learned about targeting new client segments, crafting compelling marketing campaigns, and refining her value proposition to align with the evolving needs of her business.

The chapter also covered the nuances of sales strategies, including prospecting, negotiation, and customer relationship management. Sarah was prepared to apply these strategies to attract new clients and projects.

Measuring Success

Chapter 8 concluded with a discussion on measuring success. Sarah discovered the importance of setting clear growth objectives and regularly evaluating progress against these goals. She learned to use key performance indicators (KPIs) to track her business's development and ensure that her efforts were yielding the desired results.

Sarah was excited about the potential for scaling her freelance business. She recognized that growth involved taking calculated risks, investing in resources, and embracing change. Armed with the knowledge and strategies from Chapter 8, she was determined to explore new horizons and take her gig economy entrepreneurship to the next level.

9

Navigating Challenges and Overcoming Setbacks

As Sarah's freelance business continued to grow and evolve, she knew that she would face challenges and setbacks along the way. Chapter 9 of "The Gig Economy Entrepreneur: Thriving as a Freelancer" was dedicated to helping her navigate these inevitable obstacles and emerge stronger than ever.

Identifying Common Challenges

The chapter began by outlining some of the most common challenges faced by gig economy entrepreneurs. Sarah learned that challenges could range from fluctuating income and difficult clients to work-related stress and burnout. She also understood that external factors like economic downturns and market fluctuations could impact her freelance business.

Strategies for Resilience

In the face of challenges, resilience was key. Sarah explored strategies for building resilience, which included developing a growth mindset, setting realistic expectations, and seeking support from mentors or fellow freelancers. The chapter emphasized the importance of learning from setbacks and using them as opportunities for personal and professional growth.

Client Management in Tough Times

Difficult clients or challenging projects were part of the freelance landscape. Chapter 9 provided Sarah with strategies for effectively managing such situations. She learned to set clear boundaries, communicate openly with clients, and handle disputes or conflicts professionally. The chapter also offered guidance on how to make the best of challenging projects, even when the going got tough.

Financial Survival

In times of economic uncertainty or income fluctuations, managing finances became paramount. Sarah explored strategies for financial survival, which included creating an emergency fund, diversifying income streams, and adapting her pricing and services to the market conditions. She learned to set financial goals and develop contingency plans to ensure her financial stability.

Coping with Stress and Burnout

Stress and burnout were genuine concerns for gig economy entrepreneurs who often juggled multiple roles and faced tight deadlines. The chapter introduced Sarah to stress management techniques, including mindfulness, time management, and self-care. She understood the importance of maintaining a healthy work-life balance to prevent burnout.

Learning from Setbacks

Setbacks could be valuable learning experiences. Sarah was encouraged to reflect on her challenges, identify the lessons learned, and apply those insights to her future endeavors. She realized that every obstacle she faced was an opportunity for growth and improvement.

Chapter 9 also emphasized the value of seeking support from peers, mentors, or professional networks. Sarah understood that she didn't have to face challenges alone; there was a community of freelancers who could offer guidance and encouragement.

As Sarah closed the chapter, she felt better prepared to navigate the challenges and setbacks that were an inevitable part of her gig economy journey. She had developed a resilient mindset and a toolbox of strategies to help her overcome adversity, making her even more determined to thrive as a freelance entrepreneur.

10

Leaving a Legacy and Giving Back

As Sarah continued to grow and thrive in her gig economy entrepreneurship, she was increasingly aware of the impact she could have beyond her own career. Chapter 10 of "The Gig Economy Entrepreneur: Thriving as a Freelancer" explored the themes of leaving a legacy and giving back to her community and the world.

Defining Your Legacy

The chapter began by encouraging Sarah to contemplate the legacy she wanted to leave behind. A legacy could be about more than just financial success; it could include the positive impact she made on others, the values she instilled in her work, and the mark she left on her industry.

Sarah was guided through a process of self-reflection to determine what aspects of her work and life were most important to her. By defining her legacy, she could set meaningful goals and align her actions with her long-term aspirations.

Mentorship and Paying It Forward

Sarah had benefitted from mentorship and support throughout her journey, and now, it was her turn to give back. The chapter explored the power of mentorship and how it could make a profound difference in someone else's career. Sarah learned how to become a mentor or guide to others, sharing her knowledge, experience, and wisdom.

Paying it forward went beyond mentorship. The chapter also discussed the value of giving back to the gig economy community. Sarah was introduced to the idea of contributing her expertise to freelancing forums, offering pro bono work to nonprofits, or even starting educational initiatives to help others on their freelance journey.

Corporate Social Responsibility

As her freelance business grew, Sarah was introduced to the concept of corporate social responsibility (CSR). She explored ways to integrate social and environmental responsibility into her work. The chapter provided her with insights into sustainability practices, ethical sourcing, and ways to make her business more socially conscious.

Philanthropy and Giving Back

The chapter also delved into philanthropy and charitable giving. Sarah learned how she could incorporate charitable activities into her business model, such as donating a portion of her profits to a cause she cared about. She was introduced to the benefits of philanthropy, both for the recipients and for her own sense of purpose and fulfillment.

Building a Legacy Plan

Chapter 10 concluded by helping Sarah build a legacy plan. She learned how to set specific goals and action steps to create her desired legacy, whether that involved mentorship, community involvement, or philanthropy. The chapter emphasized the importance of ongoing reflection and adjustment of her legacy plan as her career continued to evolve.

By the end of Chapter 10, Sarah was inspired to think beyond her individual success and focus on the positive impact she could make in the gig economy and the wider world. She understood that by leaving a legacy and giving back, she could create a meaningful and lasting impact while also finding personal fulfillment in her work.

11

Embracing Change and Adaptation in the Gig Economy

Sarah's journey in the gig economy had been marked by continuous growth, learning, and success. Yet, she knew that change was a constant in the modern world of freelancing. In Chapter 11 of "The Gig Economy Entrepreneur: Thriving as a Freelancer," she explored the crucial theme of embracing change and adaptation to stay relevant and successful.

The Dynamics of Change

The chapter began by discussing the rapid changes that defined the gig economy. Sarah learned that the freelancing landscape was influenced by shifts in technology, market demands, and global events. She understood that the ability to adapt to change was essential for long-term success.

Staying Relevant

To thrive in a constantly evolving environment, Sarah explored strategies for staying relevant. She learned about the value of ongoing learning, staying informed about industry trends, and continuously upgrading her skills. The chapter emphasized the importance of being agile and open to new opportunities.

Sarah also discovered the power of networking and maintaining connections with fellow freelancers and industry professionals. Staying in touch with her network could provide valuable insights and opportunities for collaboration.

Pivoting and Diversification

Pivoting was another strategy to consider in the face of change. Sarah learned how to assess when it might be necessary to pivot her services, target audience, or business model. The chapter provided her with guidance on evaluating opportunities for diversification, such as adding new services or entering different markets.

Building Resilience

Change could bring challenges and setbacks. The chapter explored resilience-building strategies, including mindset shifts and stress management techniques. Sarah was encouraged to view change as an opportunity for growth and adaptation.

Scenario Planning

The chapter emphasized the importance of scenario planning. Sarah learned to create different scenarios for her business, both positive and negative, and develop action plans for each. This strategic approach allowed her to be prepared for various outcomes and make informed decisions during periods of change.

Navigating Industry Shifts

As the gig economy evolved, it was important to anticipate and navigate industry shifts. The chapter provided Sarah with insights into analyzing industry trends, identifying emerging niches, and positioning herself to take advantage of new opportunities.

By the end of Chapter 11, Sarah felt better equipped to embrace change as an opportunity rather than a threat. She understood that in the dynamic world of the gig economy, adaptation was a key to her long-term success. Sarah was excited to continue her journey, ready to face whatever changes and challenges the future might hold.

12

Reflection and Future Horizons

As Sarah reached the final chapter of her journey as a gig economy entrepreneur, she felt a sense of accomplishment and a newfound depth of knowledge. Chapter 12 of "The Gig Economy Entrepreneur: Thriving as a Freelancer" was dedicated to reflection and charting the course for her future horizons.

Looking Back

The chapter began by encouraging Sarah to look back on her journey. She was prompted to reflect on the challenges she had overcome, the milestones she had achieved, and the lessons she had learned. Sarah understood that self-reflection was essential for personal and professional growth.

Celebrating Achievements

Sarah took the time to celebrate her achievements, both big and small. She acknowledged the successes that had shaped her journey as a freelancer. Celebrating achievements not only boosted her morale but also motivated her to set new goals and reach even higher.

Lessons Learned

Reflecting on her journey, Sarah identified the most valuable lessons she had learned along the way. Whether it was mastering pricing strategies, building her brand, or navigating challenges, each lesson had contributed to her growth and success.

Setting New Goals

With her newfound insights and experiences, Sarah was guided through the process of setting new goals. The chapter introduced her to the SMART goal-setting framework, helping her establish clear, specific, and measurable objectives for her future endeavors.

Vision for the Future

Sarah was encouraged to envision her future horizons. What did she want her freelance career to look like in the coming years? The chapter guided her through the process of defining her vision for her gig economy entrepreneurship, taking into account her aspirations, values, and long-term goals.

Legacy and Giving Back

The chapter also revisited the theme of legacy and giving back. Sarah considered how she could continue to make a positive impact in her community and industry as her career evolved. She was inspired to find new ways to leave a lasting legacy through mentorship, philanthropy, and sustainability.

Continuing Growth

Sarah understood that her journey as a gig economy entrepreneur was far from over. Chapter 12 emphasized the importance of continuing her growth, learning, and adaptation as she embarked on the next phase of her career. She recognized that the gig economy was a dynamic and evolving landscape, and staying ahead required a commitment to personal and professional development.

Gratitude and Perspective

The chapter concluded by encouraging Sarah to embrace gratitude and perspective. She was reminded to appreciate the opportunities, experiences, and connections that had enriched her journey. Gratitude and a positive perspective could provide her with the resilience and motivation to face the future with optimism and enthusiasm.

As Sarah reached the end of her journey through the pages of "The Gig Economy Entrepreneur," she was ready to embark on new adventures with a renewed sense of purpose and direction. Her reflections and goals had provided her with the roadmap for a promising and fulfilling future in the gig economy.

"The Gig Economy Entrepreneur: Thriving as a Freelancer" is a comprehensive guide that takes readers on a journey through the life of a freelancer, offering valuable insights and strategies for success in the dynamic world of the gig economy. The book is divided into twelve chapters, each addressing a different aspect of freelancing. Here is a summary of the key themes covered in each chapter:

1. Chapter 1 - "The Gig Economy Entrepreneur"
   - Introduction to the gig economy and the entrepreneurial mindset.
   - The importance of adaptability and self-reliance in freelancing.

2. Chapter 2 - "Building Your Brand"
   - Crafting a unique brand as a freelancer.

- Creating an irresistible freelance profile.
- The power of storytelling in branding.

3. Chapter 3 - "Freelance Pricing"
   - Pricing psychology and strategies.
   - Understanding the costs of freelancing.
   - Value-based pricing and different pricing models.

4. Chapter 4 - "Securing and Managing Clients"
   - Finding ideal clients and marketing strategies.
   - Effective client relationship management.
   - Time management and scaling your freelance business.

5. Chapter 5 - "Mastering Your Craft"
   - The importance of lifelong learning and professional growth.
   - Building a personal brand and sharing knowledge.
   - Setting goals and tracking progress.

6. Chapter 6 - "Financial Mastery"
   - Financial planning, budgeting, and tax management.
   - Retirement planning and investments.
   - Creating an emergency fund and insurance.

7. Chapter 7 - "Work-Life Balance and Self-Care"
   - The significance of work-life balance.
   - Strategies for setting boundaries and self-care.
   - Time management for a balanced life.

8. Chapter 8 - "Scaling Your Freelance Business"
   - The desire for growth and building a team.
   - Managing finances and operations for scaling.
   - Marketing and sales strategies for expansion.

9. Chapter 9 - "Navigating Challenges and Overcoming Setbacks"
   - Identifying common challenges and strategies for resilience.
   - Coping with stress and learning from setbacks.
   - Seeking support and mentorship.

10. Chapter 10 - "Leaving a Legacy and Giving Back"
    - Defining your legacy as a freelancer.
    - Mentorship, paying it forward, and philanthropy.
    - Integrating corporate social responsibility and ethical practices.

11. Chapter 11 - "Embracing Change and Adaptation"
    - Understanding the dynamics of change in the gig economy.
    - Staying relevant and strategies for adaptation.
    - Pivoting, building resilience, and scenario planning.

12. Chapter 12 - "Reflection and Future Horizons"
    - Looking back on the journey and celebrating achievements.
    - Setting new goals and defining a vision for the future.
    - Legacy, gratitude, and the commitment to continued growth.

"The Gig Economy Entrepreneur" is a holistic guide that equips freelancers with the knowledge, skills, and mindset needed to thrive in the gig economy. It encourages freelancers to be adaptable, resilient, and focused on long-term success, while also emphasizing the importance of giving back and making a positive impact.

www.ingramcontent.com/pod-product-compliance
Lightning Source LLC
LaVergne TN
LVHW020456080526
838202LV00057B/5983